Animal Icons
ARMADILLOS

Sheila Griffin Llanas

ABDO Publishing Company

visit us at
www.abdopublishing.com

Published by ABDO Publishing Company, PO Box 398166, Minneapolis, MN 55439.
Copyright © 2013 by Abdo Consulting Group, Inc. International copyrights reserved in all
countries. No part of this book may be reproduced in any form without written permission
from the publisher. The Checkerboard Library™ is a trademark and logo of ABDO Publishing
Company.

Printed in the United States of America, North Mankato, Minnesota.
112012
012013

 PRINTED ON RECYCLED PAPER

Cover Photo: Corbis
Interior Photos: Alamy pp. 10–11, 26–27; Getty Images pp. 4–5, 14–15, 18–19, 22–23, 24–25;
    Glow Images pp. 16–17; iStockphoto pp. 1, 9, 28–29; Joel Sartore/National Geographic Stock
    pp. 8, 12–13; Photo Researchers pp. 6–7, 20–21

Editors: Rochelle Baltzer, Megan M. Gunderson, Stephanie Hedlund
Art Direction: Neil Klinepier

Cataloging-in-Publication Data

Llanas, Sheila Griffin., 1958-
 Armadillos / Sheila Griffin Llanas.
   p. cm. -- (Animal icons)
Includes bibliographical references and index.
ISBN 978-1-61783-567-4
1. Armadillos--Juvenile literature. I. Title.
599.3/12--dc22

2012946533

CONTENTS

ARMADILLOS

One night, a Florida homeowner walked out into her yard. She heard a snuffling sound and leaves rustling. She looked and saw an armadillo right at her feet!

The armadillo kept its nose down and continued **foraging** for bugs. The woman stood still as the armadillo came closer. Focused on its food, it bumped into her toes!

Armadillos, or 'dillos, live in North, Central, and South America. There are 20 known species. But only the nine-banded armadillo lives in the United States. It has the biggest population and the largest **habitat** of all armadillo species. It is the only mammal in the United States that has a true shell.

The nine-banded armadillo came to Texas in the 1800s. It quickly became part of Texas **culture**. From there, it extended its range.

The armadillo is one of a kind. To some, it is ugly. To others, it is adorable. In Texas, it is famous. But this shy, **nocturnal** loner just wants to stay out of trouble. The amazing armadillo is an animal icon.

An icon is a cultural symbol. Animal icons stand for the people and land of nations, states, and cities. Animal icons are shown on flags and signs. They appear in songs, legends, and stories. They represent history. They teach people about nature and about themselves.

5

ARMADILLO HISTORY

Armadillos look downright prehistoric. That's because their ancient relatives were glyptodonts. Glyptodonts were as big as rhinoceroses! These creatures lived during the Pleistocene epoch, which was 2.6 million to 11,700 years ago.

Glyptodonts lived in the area that would become Texas. Some weighed two tons (2 t). These giants have been extinct for thousands of years.

Another ancient armadillo relative lived in the Midwest. The beautiful armadillo, or *Dasypus bellus*, was three times larger than the nine-banded armadillo. This species also went extinct. So for thousands of years, no armadillos lived in the United States.

Fun modern species names include pink fairy armadillo and screaming hairy armadillo.

Today, the largest armadillo species is the giant armadillo of South America. It can be up to 39 inches (99 cm) long and weigh up to 132 pounds (60 kg)!

Finally in the mid-1800s, the nine-banded armadillo entered Texas. People traveling north across the Rio Grande may have brought live armadillos as a food source. Soon, armadillos were on their way to other states.

By 1921, the nine-banded armadillo's range extended into Arkansas. Next, armadillos began living in Florida. Supposedly, they originally escaped from a Florida zoo! Next, armadillos moved into Louisiana and Oklahoma.

Armadillos were very successful at **migrating** across the United States. Truckers and travelers may have helped transport them. Armadillos also hopped on cattle cars to cross the miles by train.

Armadillos are not territorial.
Their home ranges overlap.

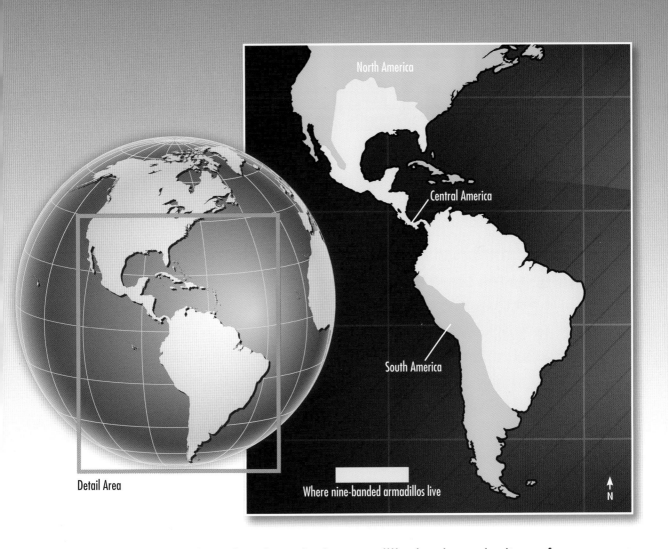

Detail Area

Central America

North America

South America

Where nine-banded armadillos live

N

By 1995, the nine-banded armadillo had made it as far as Missouri and Illinois. Today, the only thing stopping the armadillo's journey north is cold weather. They have not learned how to survive the harsh northern winters.

MORE LORE

Armadillos are popular in myths and stories. A Mayan legend tells of the Sun wanting to teach two gods a lesson. He has them sit on a bench in front of all the other gods. The bench turns into a pair of armadillos, which jump into the air. The two gods fall off in disgrace.

An ancient story from Mexico associates the armadillo with the earth because the animal burrows. In Argentina, three armadillo myths tell of the origins of women, agriculture, and fire.

When Spanish conquistador Hernán Cortés explored Mexico in the 1500s, he saw armadillos. He gave them their name, which is Spanish for "little armored thing."

Naturalist John James Audubon is best known for his drawings of birds. But he also drew the armadillo in the mid-1800s. Many people had never seen this special mammal. He described it as a combination of a pig and a turtle!

Armadillos also are featured in Rudyard Kipling's *Just So Stories*. In "The Beginning of

During the Great Depression, Texans cooked and ate armadillos. They called them "poor man's pork" and "Texas turkey."

the Armadilloes," Stickly-Prickly Hedgehog and Slow-Solid Tortoise trick Painted Jaguar. They combine their best features. Tortoise's shell becomes **flexible**. Hedgehog's prickles turn into armor. Jaguar is confused and calls them a new name, armadillo!

PLATE TO PLATE

Armadillos are not like any other animals! They are not reptiles, turtles, hedgehogs, or opossums. Armadillos are mammals. Their closest relatives are sloths and anteaters.

The nine-banded armadillo's scientific name is *Dasypus novemcinctus*. This species is also known as the long-nosed armadillo and the Texas armadillo. It has a small head with a long snout and pointy ears. Sparse yellow hair covers the armadillo's tender belly. Besides that, the armadillo has little hair.

The armadillo's main feature is its armor. The **carapace** is a set of plates that covers the animal's body. It is brown to yellowish white. It is covered in scales that are yellowish tan or gray.

The nine-banded armadillo gets its name from the movable bands in the middle of its **carapace**. However, this species can have 8 to 11 movable bands. Skin between the bands gives the armadillo **flexibility** so it can bend and twist its body.

The carapace protects armadillos from some predators. However, it does not protect them from cold weather. Armadillos have almost no body fat. In addition, they have a low body temperature. So, they cannot survive cold winters.

Dasypus *means "tortoise-rabbit."*
Novemcinctus *means "nine bands."*

Armadillos are bigger than you might think! They weigh 12 to 17 pounds (5 to 8 kg). They grow to be 30 inches (76 cm) long. The tail can be 14 to 16 inches (36 to 41 cm) of that length. Ten or more bands let them move this long tail.

The armadillo's food is found right under its nose. So, it relies on a strong sense of smell. The armadillo also has strong legs and long claws for digging. And, it has a long, sticky tongue for slurping up food.

The armadillo has peg-shaped teeth. Unlike your teeth, these do not have **enamel**. They are only good for crushing food. And, they are only in the back of the animal's mouth. An armadillo could not bite a predator if it tried!

To get out of harm's way, armadillos may run away. They can run pretty fast on their four short legs. Each front foot has four toes. The hind feet each have five toes. Armadillos walk on the tips of their feet. So, their footprints look like bird tracks.

Armadillos make a buzzing noise when they run fast. They have been known to outrun dogs and hunters. When people do catch armadillos, they notice these animals are stinky! Still, some people keep them as pets.

Armadillos have poor eyesight. Luckily, they don't need sharp eyes to find their food.

WHAT'S FOR DINNER?

Armadillos are insectivores. They eat ants, beetles, grubs, centipedes, millipedes, and earthworms. Armadillos also eat insect larvae and spiders.

Without enough bugs to eat, an armadillo will expand its menu. It will eat plants, fungi, berries, fruits, eggs, and **carrion**. But mostly, an armadillo's dinner is all about bugs.

Sometimes, this habit is helpful. Armadillos do humans a favor by eating pests. They eat fire ants, which can cause painful stings. They also eat grubs, which can damage lawns. Unfortunately, armadillos have to dig up lawns and gardens to get at them!

When they are awake, nine-banded armadillos **forage** constantly. They walk with their noses to the ground, sniffing for underground bugs. Absorbed in foraging, they forget to look around. They can even bump into other animals!

A foraging armadillo may pause and rear up on its hind legs. It sniffs the air and moves its head from side to side. Its tail helps it balance.

17

When armadillos find food, they do not like to work hard to get it. They are not fighters. They do not want to attack a meal. They prefer digging in soft soils with their large claws. Then, they stick out their long tongues and lick up the bugs.

It takes a lot of spit to lick up all those bugs. Luckily, the nine-banded armadillo has a **unique** salivary bladder full of thick saliva. How it works is simple. The armadillo smells bugs to eat. Then, the muscles over its bladder contract. This makes sticky saliva squirt out onto its tongue.

Armadillos are noisy eaters. They grunt while foraging!

Armadillos lap up water with their tongues like dogs.

The armadillo's tongue is not just for catching insects. It is also for quenching thirst. Armadillos drink a lot of water. On the water's surface, they leave behind a film of saliva. Gross!

ARMADILLO BEHAVIOR

The armadillo's favorite **habitats** are warm grasslands, woods, brush, and scrubland. Armadillos live in underground burrows. They prefer soft, sandy soil that is easy to dig. So, they like to live near lakes, rivers, or places with good rainfall.

Armadillos are **nocturnal**. During the day, they sleep in their burrows. To build this home, an armadillo digs an entrance that is seven inches (17 cm) wide. This leads to a long tunnel. It ends in a wider sleeping area.

An armadillo hauls plants into its sleeping area to make a cozy bed. It holds leaves and grass with its front legs and nose while shuffling backward. The armadillo uses its tail to guide itself into the burrow.

Armadillos sleep for up to 17 hours a day. Yet other animals also use armadillo burrows. Rabbits, rats, opossums, skunks, insects, and spiders all find homes there.

An armadillo burrow can have several entrances.

Sometimes, armadillos make nests outside of burrows.

Armadillos are eaten by other carnivores. They must watch out for dogs, wild cats, foxes, alligators, raccoons, bears, and birds of prey. Humans hunt and eat them, too. Humans also poison armadillos where they are considered pests.

The nine-banded armadillo has several ways to escape danger. It can play dead or run away. Or, it can find or dig a burrow to hide in. An armadillo will wedge into a burrow and arch its back. Then it's almost impossible to get it out!

The armadillo also has a **unique** way of scaring enemies. It can jump up into the air! Hopefully, this will surprise a predator and give the armadillo a few seconds to run away.

Armadillos can also escape by plunging into water. They are good swimmers. They suck in air to inflate their **digestive** systems. Then they float and dog-paddle across the water.

Armadillos can also sink and walk across the bottom of a river or a pond. They can hold their breath for six minutes or more!

Sometimes, armadillos cannot escape. If they have to fight, they scratch with their claws. But armadillos prefer to sleep and eat bugs instead.

The nine-banded armadillo does not curl into a ball. Only the three-banded armadillo does that for protection.

Nine-banded armadillos can jump three to four feet (0.9 to 1.2 m) into the air!

BIRTH TO DEATH

Armadillos mate between June and August. After mating, the couple does not stay together. When ready, the female decides to become **pregnant**. She often waits up to four months. She wants conditions to be good for raising her pups.

Four months after becoming pregnant, the mother gives birth to four identical pups. Each newborn weighs just three to four ounces (85 to 114 g). It has a thin, soft **carapace**. This hardens within a few days. An armadillo pup walks within a few hours of birth.

Like other mammals, the mother nurses her pups. After two to three months, the pups leave the burrow with

Nine-banded armadillos almost always have quadruplets.

their mother. The pups learn by watching her. When she sniffs for bugs, they sniff for bugs.

Pups are **weaned** by five months. Armadillos become fully mature when they are about a year old. The nine-banded armadillo's life span is 12 to 15 years.

THE ICONIC ARMADILLO

The armadillo has been an icon in American **culture** for many years. In the late 1960s, it appealed to college students and young adults. At the time, many students protested war. The shy, passive armadillo was a good symbol for them to use.

In the 1970s, armadillo racing became popular. Around the same time, Texas artist Jim Franklin became the "Michelangelo of armadillo art." He decorated the Armadillo World Headquarters, which is a music hall in Austin.

In 1972, Northwestern University in Texas held its first Armadillo Day. 'Dillo

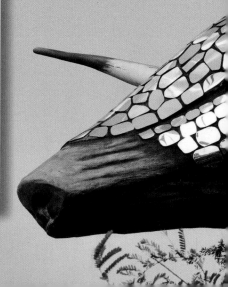

A huge armadillo sits outside a restaurant in Houston, Texas. Oddly, this roadside attraction has the horns of a steer!

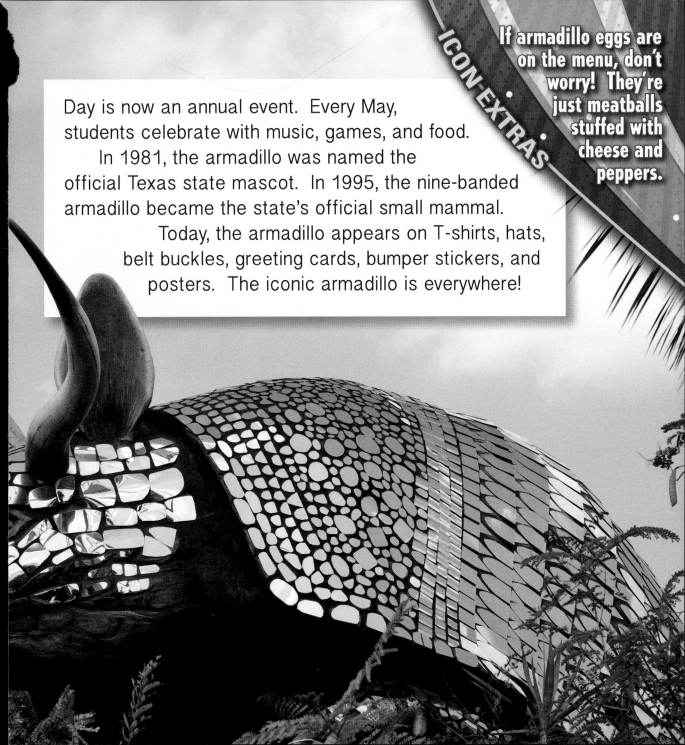

Day is now an annual event. Every May, students celebrate with music, games, and food.

In 1981, the armadillo was named the official Texas state mascot. In 1995, the nine-banded armadillo became the state's official small mammal.

Today, the armadillo appears on T-shirts, hats, belt buckles, greeting cards, bumper stickers, and posters. The iconic armadillo is everywhere!

INTO THE FUTURE

Today, experts think 30 to 50 million armadillos live in the United States. The **IUCN** lists armadillos as "least concern." They are not endangered. In fact, their population and range are growing!

People who live near armadillos face a tough situation. Some think armadillos are useful. They kill many insect pests. Others think armadillos are pests themselves. They dig up yards and gardens in their search for food.

In the future, armadillos may **migrate** farther north. They could even survive in parts of Canada! Armadillos do not **hibernate**, so they need a food source available year-round. That means the only thing stopping them is cold weather.

Armadillo **migration** continues to fascinate scientists. In just 150 years, the little armadillo has come a long way!

Armadillos tend to be slow, so their biggest nightmare is crossing a road. They cannot get out of the way fast enough to avoid oncoming traffic. Or, they jump when startled and are killed by vehicles.

GLOSSARY

carapace (KEHR-uh-pays) - a shell or bony case or shield covering the back of an animal.

carrion - dead, rotting flesh.

culture - the customs, arts, and tools of a nation or a people at a certain time.

digestive - of or relating to the breakdown of food into simpler substances the body can absorb.

enamel - a hard substance that forms a thin outer layer on teeth.

flexibility - the ability to bend or move easily.

forage - to search.

habitat - a place where a living thing is naturally found.

hibernate - to spend a period of time, such as the winter, in deep sleep.

IUCN - the International Union for Conservation of Nature. The IUCN is a global environmental organization focused on conservation.

migrate - to move from one place to another, often to find food.

nocturnal - active at night.

pregnant - having one or more babies growing within the body.

unique - being the only one of its kind.

wean - to accustom an animal to eating food other than its mother's milk.

WEB SITES

To learn more about armadillos, visit ABDO Publishing Company online. Web sites about armadillos are featured on our Book Links page. These links are routinely monitored and updated to provide the most current information available.

www.abdopublishing.com

INDEX